D1161156

Oil Worker

BY MIRELLA S. MILLER

Published in the United States of America by The Child's World®
1980 Lookout Drive • Mankato, MN 56003-1705
800-599-READ • www.childsworld.com

Acknowledgments
The Child's World®: Mary Berendes, Publishing Director
Red Line Editorial: Editorial direction
The Design Lab: Design
Amnet: Production

Photographs ©: Shutterstock Images, cover, 6, 17; Thinkstock, 5,
15; Andrey Armyagov/Shutterstock Images, 8; Neal Ulevich/
AP Images, 11; Gaylon Wampler/Corbis, 13; Jerry Burnes/AP
Images, 18; Fluke Samed/Shutterstock Images, 20

ISBN 9781631436901
LCCN 2014945302

Printed in the United States of America
Mankato, MN
November, 2014
PA02238

ABOUT THE AUTHOR

Mirella S. Miller is an author and editor. She lives in Minnesota with her husband and dog.

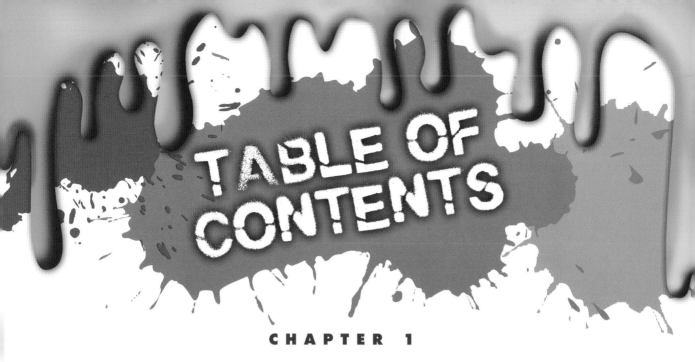

TABLE OF CONTENTS

CHAPTER 1

What Does an Oil Worker Do?

Oil, also called **petroleum**, is a natural liquid found under Earth's surface. It often looks like black sludge. More than 3 billion gallons (11 billion L) of oil is used worldwide daily. Oil is used to make gasoline and plastic products. It is also used for heating and electric power. The United States uses more oil than any other nation.

Since petroleum is found below ground, oil workers must drill for it. Oil workers work in **oil fields** in places where oil is found. Oil fields are like tiny towns. They have buildings where workers live when they are on site. They have places for workers to eat and use the bathroom. Oil fields are covered in towers called derricks that hold big drills. Workers use these drills to get down to the oil deep beneath the Earth. Once they get the oil out, workers

Petroleum comes in many different colors and consistencies, but the most familiar is thick and black.

transport the oil to **refineries** where it is made into gasoline and other products.

Oil is also found beneath the ocean. Some oil workers work on big platforms in the ocean called oil **rigs**. Ocean oil rigs are like floating cities. Ocean oil workers live on the rigs for days or weeks at a time. Then they have days or weeks off. There are private rooms, gyms, and cafeterias for the workers. Rigs either float or are attached to the ocean floor. These rigs

Oil rigs have to bring petroleum up through water and rock.

allow oil to be extracted from places where humans could not get it otherwise. The platforms have facilities to store the oil until it can be transported to shore.

Oil workers fill many different roles. They work together to bring oil to the surface. Drillers work the drills that dig the wells. They also train workers and make sure all safety rules are followed. Pumpers use machines to pump oil out from the wells. Engine operators keep power running on the platform. Derrick operators repair pumps and make sure all the rig equipment is working. Roustabouts repair machines, keep work spaces clean, operate cranes to move heavy equipment around, and help out wherever they are needed. Each platform has a few **welders** working. They fix everyday problems with the rig. They also help build new metalwork. Welders have one of the busiest jobs on a rig. But every worker is needed to make the rig work.

Oil workers work even in rain and snow. They work on platforms high above the ground. This is why it is important for workers to follow safety rules.

Oil workers' gear does not always keep them from getting dirty.

8

Oil fields and oil rigs are noisy places. The machines are very loud. Oil workers must wear earplugs to prevent hearing loss. They communicate with other workers using hand signals. Along with earplugs, most oil workers need to wear hard hats and steel-toed boots. These help protect workers if any objects fall. Workers also wear jumpsuits. Drilling for oil is a messy job. Most workers are covered in grease at the end of the day. Oil fields and rigs smell of gas. It is a strong, bad smell.

CHAPTER 2

A Day on the Job

Before working a platform, oil workers must go through a lot of training. They learn how to use the heavy equipment. There are also a lot of safety rules to learn.

Oil platforms have people working at all hours of the day. This means more oil is produced. More oil means more money for a company. Many workers work for two weeks at once. Then the worker gets one to three weeks off. This time off helps the workers rest from their hard work.

Oil workers often work 12-hour shifts during the

TECHNOLOGY

Oil drilling is constantly changing. The oil industry is developing new ways of drilling, including drilling horizontally under the ground. This helps them reach areas without disturbing the ground above. Oil companies have also begun developing lasers to drill oil wells.

Women repair equipment in the Shengli oil field in China.

day or at night. Each shift begins with a big meal. Workers need energy to work for long periods of time. After they eat, they go to do their work. Sometimes weather or broken equipment changes a rig's schedule. Every day is different on a rig.

Oil workers drill a lot of wells. Roustabouts move pipes through the platform. Then derrick operators help guide the pipes into place. The pipes pull the oil up from the ground. Once the pipes are in place, derrick operators listen for any funny sounds from the pipe. These noises could mean something is wrong. The ground of a platform can be slippery. It is important for roustabouts to clean up the mud so that no one slips.

Mud engineers are also busy. They create and monitor a substance called drilling mud. There are different types of drilling mud. But most mud is made of water, clay, and a mixture of chemicals. It looks like a chocolate milk shake. Drilling mud is pumped into the well as it is dug. The mud carries cut pieces of rock to the surface so they don't get in the way of the drill. The heavy mud also keeps outside fluids out of the well. This prevents the well from blowing out and spewing oil above the surface in a gusher. Engineers test

the mud regularly to make sure its weight and other properties are what the well needs.

No matter their job, oil workers must be ready to work hard. Their work is important to provide fuel for the world's machines and material for its products.

DISGUSTING!

If pipes are not connected correctly, mud can spray everywhere. Oil workers and their work area get covered in mud. This mud is a mixture of water, crude oil, and gas.

CHAPTER 3

Why Oil Matters

Without oil, planes, cars, and trucks could not travel. It would be hard to heat houses and buildings. And many medicines and products with plastic could not be made.

The oil and gas industries also provide many jobs for people. As of 2014, the North Dakota oil boom that started in 2006 had created more than 30,000 jobs. At the same time, the petroleum industry directly employed more than 200,000 people in the United States alone.

TECHNOLOGY

Oil companies used to search for oil by drilling many test wells to see if oil was present. This practice damaged land and ocean habitats. Now oil companies can use satellites and airplanes to find oil underground by sensing changes in the Earth's gravitational and magnetic fields. These methods do far less damage. Drilling only takes place when oil companies are confident there is oil to be found.

Most cars on the road are powered by gasoline made from petroleum.

CHAPTER 4

Overcoming Problems

Oil workers face many problems on the job. They must follow many kinds of rules. Some rules help keep workers safe. Other rules help protect the area. Even when everyone is careful, things can go wrong.

Oil workers use heavy machinery. If workers are not careful, they can hurt themselves or others with these machines. Large metal pipes are moved around a lot. If workers are not paying attention when pipes are moving, they could be hit. This is why workers must be aware. They must look at other workers and communicate.

Explosions and fires are rare, but they sometimes happen on oil rigs. Since oil catches on fire easily, oil rigs are designed with fire prevention in mind. Workers avoid making any kind of spark or flame on an oil rig. Any spark

A worker checks a pump in an oil field.

can start a fire or cause gas to explode. If a fire happens, workers know how to react. They follow procedures to stay safe and put out any fires immediately.

A worker cleans mud off equipment on a drilling rig.

Along with following safety rules on an oil rig, workers must wear proper gear. Oil workers wear jumpsuits. This keeps oil and grease from getting on their clothes. The jumpsuits are meant to get dirty. Many oil workers must also wear hard hats. This keeps a worker's head safe from heavy objects. Steel-toed boots are sturdy. They keep workers' toes from getting crunched. When the platform gets wet, these boots keep workers from slipping. Oil workers wear safety glasses. These protect a worker's eyes when oil or mud sprays.

Oil platforms are usually high off the ground. Oil workers that work near the edge of the platform wear safety harnesses. This keeps them safe if they fall.

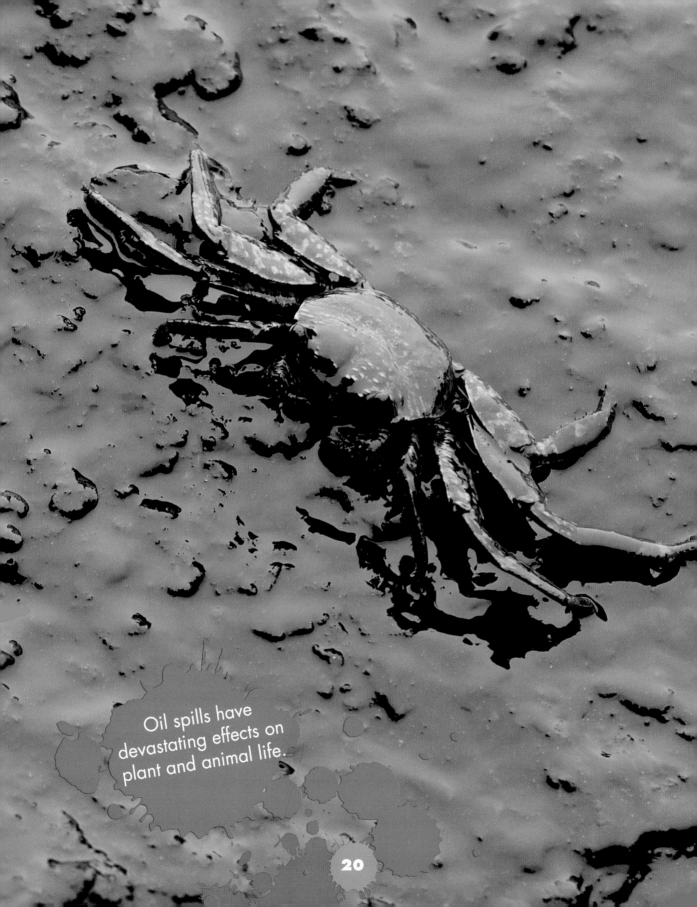

Oil spills have devastating effects on plant and animal life.

Oil workers work hard to prevent oil spills. Spills are caused by bad weather, faulty equipment, or worker error. If a lot of oil spills, it can harm animals and plants living in an ocean near the rig or on land near the field. The oil can hurt or kill animals and plants. Oil spills are hard to clean up. So oil workers try to stop them from happening. They follow safety rules to reduce risk. They make sure their machines are working properly. They practice what to do in an emergency.

DISGUSTING!
In 1989 an oil spill in Alaska dumped 11 million gallons (42 million L) of oil into the ocean. That equals 430 classrooms full of oil!

It is a lot of work to get petroleum from the ground to refineries. But we need it to fuel our cars, make plastic products, and produce electricity. To do all that, we need oil workers who are willing to get dirty.

GLOSSARY

oil fields (OIL FEELDZ) Oil fields are areas where there is a lot of oil and where equipment has been set up to remove it from the ground. Countries with a lot of oil, such as Saudi Arabia, Russia, and the United States, have many oil fields.

petroleum (puh-TROH-lee-uhm) Petroleum is a fuel source that comes from below the ground. Petroleum is used to make gasoline and other products.

refineries (ri-FYE-nur-eez) Refineries are places where the unwanted substances in something are removed. Petroleum is pulled from the ground and moved to refineries to create gasoline.

rigs (RIGZ) Rigs are equipment or machinery fitted for a special purpose. Oil companies build oil rigs in the ocean.

welders (WELL-durz) Welders are people whose job it is to join pieces of metal together. A few welders work on every oil platform.

TO LEARN MORE

BOOKS

Thomas, William David. *Oil Rig Worker*. Tarrytown, NY: Marshall Cavendish, 2011.

White, Katherine. *Oil Rig Workers: Life Drilling for Oil*. New York: Rosen Publishing, 2003.

WEB SITES

Visit our Web site for links about oil workers:
childsworld.com/links

Note to Parents, Teachers, and Librarians: We routinely verify our Web links to make sure they are safe and active sites. So encourage your readers to check them out!

INDEX

DATE DUE

			PRINTED IN U.S.A.